PEDAL POWER!

Land's End to John o'Groats in 26 days

C000214409

written by Jenny Alexander

illustrated by Jeff Anderson

Contents

Last summer, my family cycled from Land's End to John o' Groats. They are the two places in mainland Britain which are furthest apart, and the distance between them is 1,406 km in a straight line.

We had to prepare for the trip, building up our fitness through training rides every weekend. We planned a route that would take us on minor roads as much as possible, and avoid most of the major cities. We decided not to try to do more than 80 or 90 km a day, with several rest days in between. We stayed in youth hostels whenever we could.

John o' Groats

Tongue
26
25
Carbisdale Castle
24
Forres
Inverness 22 21
Loch Ness Tomintoul
23 20
Braemar
19
18
Perth
17
16 Edinburgh
15
Yarrowford
14
Annan
13
Dufton
12
Slaidburn
11 10
Manchester
Broomedge
9
Great Bolas
8
Leominster
7
St Briavels
6
Cardiff
5
Cheddar Gorge
Exford
Street
3 4
Bude
2
1 Perranporth
Land's End

Scale
0   100   200 km

N
W   E
S

JOHN O'GROATS
Lands End 874   Pentland Stories 6
ORKNEY & SHETLAND ISLES

LANDS END
NEW YORK 3147   JOHN O'GROATS 874
ISLES OF SCILLY 28   LONGSHIP LIGHTHOUSE 1½

London

3

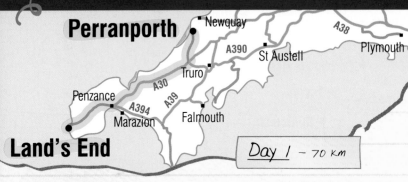

Perranporth • Newquay
A38
A390 St Austell
Plymouth
Truro
A30
Penzance A39
A394
Marazion Falmouth

Land's End

The rock arches at Perr

Day 1 – 70 km

I thought Land's End was going to be really wild and
rugged, so I was disappointed to find there was a big
visitor centre there. We had our photo taken beside the
famous signpost and then set off towards Penzance.
The countryside was flat and open, dotted with farms
and small holiday parks.

Land's End Visitor Centre

The ride from Marazion on the
south coast to Perranporth on
north coast took us along miles
Cornwall's typical narrow countr
lanes with high hedges.

Near the coast, the countryside
opens out again and we had a lo
downhill run into Perranporth.

We ate Cornish pasties on the
sandy beach.

Bude
Holsworthy
Hatherleigh
Okehampton
M5
A39 Launceston
A386
A30
Exeter
Wadebridge
Tavistock
Dartmoor
Dawlish
vquay Bodmin A38
Plymouth
A38
Torquay
Perranporth

Total:
163 km

Day 2 – 93 km

On the rolling hills at St Breock Downs, we passed
right by a wind farm. We had seen others in the
distance, but we didn't realise how tall the wind
turbines were, or what a whirring noise they made.

Between Wadebridge and Bude, the coastline is very
rugged and hilly, except for the wide sandy beach at
Widemouth Bay. At one point the road is marked 1:3,
and we all had to get off and walk. Even then, I
could hardly manage to push my bike, it was so steep.

When we got to Bude, we had a Cornish cream tea
and watched the surfers out in the bay.

The rugged coastline of North Cornwall

The windmills are 35
metres tall and their
blades are 37 metres
in diameter.

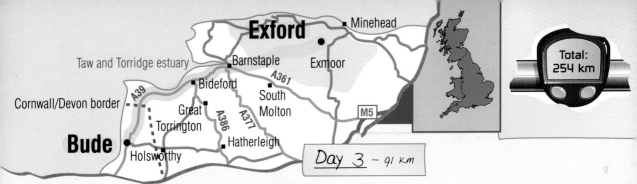

Minehead
Exford
Barnstaple
Taw and Torridge estuary
Exmoor
A361
Bideford
Cornwall/Devon border
A39
Great
Torrington
A386
South
Molton
A377
M5
Bude
Holsworthy
Hatherleigh

Total:
254 km

Day 3 - 91 km

Today we crossed from Cornwall
into Devon. The lanes were a bit
wider and straighter, and they
took us through rolling farmland
with lots of cows and sheep.

The Tarka Trail

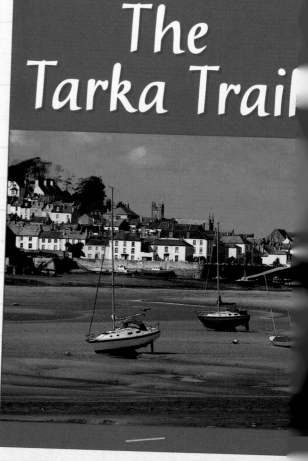

We followed the Tarka Trail cycle
track from Bideford to Barnstaple
along the Taw and Torridge estuary,
which is wide and flat so the cycling
was easy.

But after Barnstaple we had a
steady climb up on to Exmoor. There
were lots of high hills, with plenty of
bracken and very few trees.

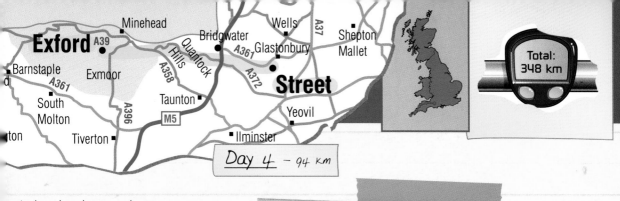

Minehead
Exford A39
Barnstaple
A361
Exmoor
South
Molton
Tiverton
Bridgwater
A361
Glastonbury
Wells
A37
Shepton
Mallet
Street
A372
Taunton
Yeovil
Ilminster
M5
A396
A358
Quantock Hills
A37

Total: 348 km

Day 4 – 94 km

We started with a lovely long downhill run off of Exmoor, and then went up over the Quantock Hills towards Bridgwater.

The Somerset Levels

I got my first puncture on Exmoor.

After that we had a great ride across the Somerset Levels which is *marshland* criss-crossed with long straight drainage ditches, so the lanes are straight and flat.

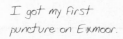

Wigeon and heron are found in the area.

Day 5 – rest day

Cheddar Gorge is the biggest
gorge in Britain. The cliffs on
each side are about 130 metres
high. We walked along the road
at the bottom, and then went
up through the woods and back
along the top.

COME AND VISIT
CHEDDAR GORGE!

stalactites

The best bit for me was
going in the caves, especially
Cox's Cave because it had
such wonderful stalactites
and stalagmites.

stalac

stala

Day 6 - 94 km

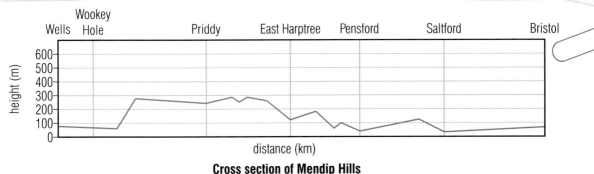

| | Wookey | | Priddy | East Harptree | Pensford | Saltford | Bristol |

height (m)
600
500
400
300
200
100
0

distance (km)

Cross section of Mendip Hills

Mud flats at the Severn estuary with the old
Severn bridge in the background.

We went over the Mendips today.
You really notice how many hills there
are in England when you're on a cycle
tour! They've got wooded valleys and
open farmland on the hilltops.

We went south of Bristol, past
Avonmouth and along the Severn estuary.
The river is very wide, with mud flats,
and the whole area is very industrial.
There are old factories as well as new
ones, and we were very aware of the
noise of traffic on the motorways nearby.

We passed the new Severn bridge and
crossed the river on the old one, which
was built in the 1960s. On the other side
the land became *rural* and hilly again.

The new Severn bridge

English and
Welsh Border

• **Leominster**

Hay-on-Wye

A49

M5

Brecon

• Hereford

Abergavenny

M50

• Tewkesbury

A466

• Cheltenham

Gloucester

St Briavels

Total:
524 km

Day 7 – 82 km

Offa's Dyke runs past St Briavels and through the
Welsh Marches along the length of the Welsh border.

We cycled up through the
Welsh Marches today, near
the border between England
and Wales. The first part
of the ride was in the
Forest of Dean, so it was
very wooded but we kept
getting glimpses of the
River Wye through the trees.

When we left the forest,
the country lanes took us
through miles of peaceful
rolling farmland. We got to
Leominster (pronounced
"Lemster") quite early and
had a look round. The
whole area is famous for
its very old black and
white houses.

Some of these houses are 600 years old.

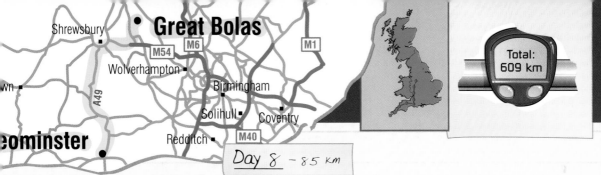

Shrewsbury
Great Bolas
Wolverhampton
Birmingham
Solihull
Coventry
Redditch
wn
eominster

Total: 609 km

Day 8 – 85 km

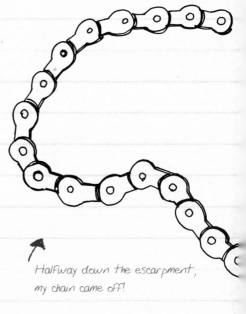

Halfway down the escarpment, my chain came off!

Today we cycled up the long hill to the top of Wenlock Edge, which is the finest escarpment in Britain. We went along the top, and then down the other side, which was steep and wooded. From the top, we had a great view of the surrounding countryside, and from the bottom we could see the whole long sweep of the escarpment.

Wenlock Edge

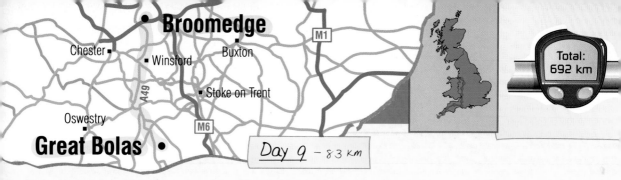

• **Broomedge**

Chester ▪   Buxton
    • Winsford

        ▪ Stoke on Trent

Oswestry
▪
Great Bolas •

Day 9 – 83 km

Total:
692 km

Crossing the Cheshire Plain was fast and easy because it is so flat and the roads were straight. But after Winsford, our surroundings got much more built-up. The area was very industrial with lots of roads and factories.

Cycling wasn't much fun, because of the fumes from so much traffic, but we still saw lots of other cyclists.

Across the Cheshire Plain you can see for miles.

The Manchester Ship Canal

Day 10 – rest day

The Manchester Ship Canal

We went for a walk along the
Manchester Ship Canal. In the old
days it would have been full of cargo
boats carrying goods from the
factories to the sea ports, and it
must have looked very strange, seeing
quite big ships sailing so far inland.

The Manchester Ship Canal is
56 km long, between
Eastham and Salford.

Lancaster

Leeds

Liverpool

Manchester
Salford

Eastham

Chester

13

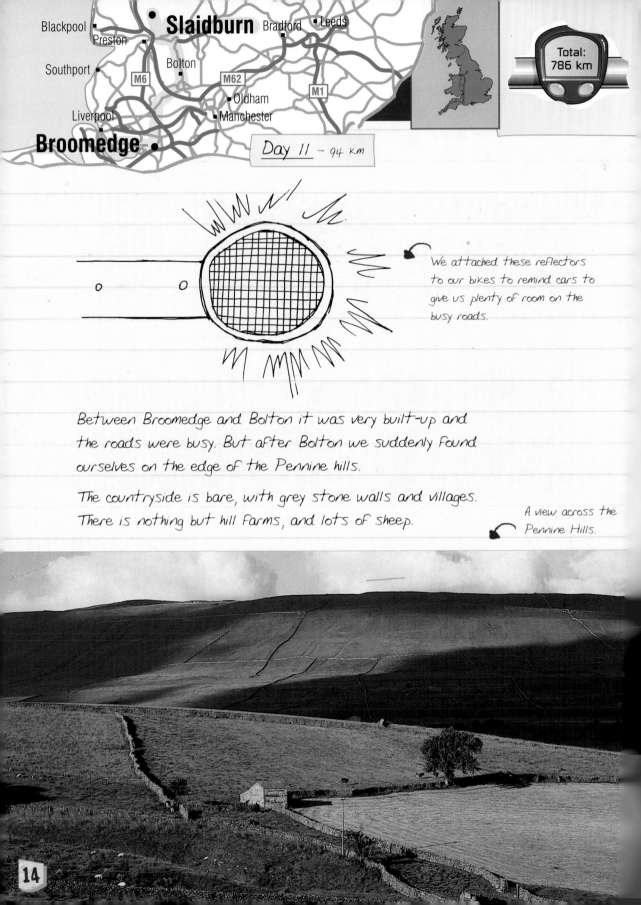

Blackpool
Slaidburn
Bradford
Leeds
Preston
Southport
Bolton
M6
M62
M1
Oldham
Manchester
Liverpool
Broomedge

Total:
786 km

Day 11 - 94 km

We attached these reflectors
to our bikes to remind cars to
give us plenty of room on the
busy roads.

Between Broomedge and Bolton it was very built-up and
the roads were busy. But after Bolton we suddenly found
ourselves on the edge of the Pennine hills.

The countryside is bare, with grey stone walls and villages.
There is nothing but hill farms, and lots of sheep.

A view across the
Pennine Hills.

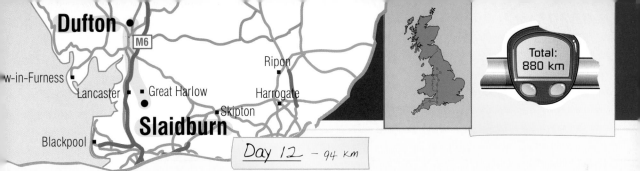

Dufton •

[M6]

w-in-Furness

Lancaster   • Great Harlow

Ripon

Harrogate

• Skipton

Slaidburn

Blackpool

Total: 880 km

Day 12 – 94 km

We started with a big climb over Great Harlow, which is in the forest of Bowland. There are no houses or villages for miles, and the weather was bad, with thick mist and rain. Some of the roads have got gates across them.

Great Harlow is 450m high – that's one and a half Eiffel Towers.

The forest of Bowland isn't really a forest but high empty moorland.

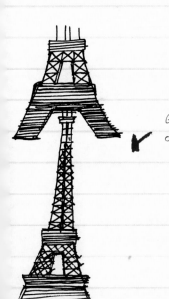

There wasn't anywhere to have lunch, so we had a picnic, but we all got cold because we couldn't find any shelter. Dad said he wouldn't like to be cycling across there on his own, because if you fell off you could be lying in a ditch for days and nobody would find you.

At the youth hostel, we met several walkers, because Dufton is on the Pennine Way. Some of them had a competition to see who had the biggest blisters!

Annan•
Gretna
Alston
Durham
Solway Firth
Workington •
Barnard Castle
Egremont •
Ravenglass • **Dufton** • M6

Total: 965 km

Day 13 – 85 km

The Solway Firth.

We cycled along the edge of the Pennines, with farmland on our left and hills on our right. The countryside got flatter and more open around the Solway Firth. It was so windy, I could hardly stay on my bike. Most of the fields were full of cows.

Just before Gretna, we crossed the border into Scotland. We had haggis and chips for tea.

Haggis and chips.

Yarrowford

M74(M)

Jedburgh

Moffat

A7

A68

Lockerbie

Otterburn

Amble

Dumfries

Annan

Whitley Bay

Total: 1,037 km

Day 14 - 72 km

We could go really fast on the flat roads, so I had a race with my sister. I nearly won, but I got a puncture!

We had an easy start to the day, because it was flat farming country as far as Lockerbie. After that we cycled across miles and miles of empty uplands, with no villages and hardly any traffic on the roads.

There were broad valleys with wide, stony rivers, and gentle rolling hills. Most of the valleys were farmed, but the hilltops were either bare or covered with plantations of fir trees.

I got another puncture just after we'd set off.

17

Edinburgh

Livingston

M9

Dalkeith

M8

Motherwell

A7

A68

A702

Moorfoot Hills

Yarrowford

Day 15 – 80 km

From the top of the
Moorfoot Hills we had a
brilliant view of Edinburgh
and the Firth of Forth. We
cycled down into the city.
It has got tall grey stone
houses and wide streets.

Our view
of Edinburgh

The city centre was busy, so
we got off and pushed our
bikes down Princes Street.

Dunblane

Stirling

Dunfermline

Firth of Forth

Dunbar

Edinburgh

Livingston

Dalkeith

Glasgow

Motherwell

M9

M8

A80

A702

B11

Day 16 — rest day

First we visited the castle. It is on the site of an extinct volcano, and Castle Rock is actually a volcanic plug.

The castle

After that we went up Arthur's Seat and along the Salisbury Crags. It was odd to find such a steep, high hill in the middle of a big city. The view from the top was well worth the climb.

Salisbury Crags

Day 17 – 80 km

The Edinburgh cycle route took us out of the city on minor roads and disused railway lines. We passed huge houses in wide suburban streets, with high-rise flats close by.

The road to the Forth Road Bridge is flat. We crossed on the special track for cyclists and walkers. It's a suspension bridge like the old Severn bridge. To our right, we could see the rail bridge, which looked quite different, much heavier and more solid.

On the other side we came into coal mining country. It felt quite industrial, but with lots of green spaces and empty hills all around.

After that it was fairly flat cycling up to Perth.

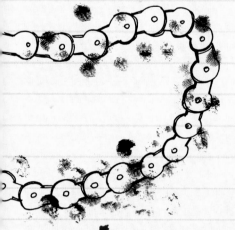

My bike chain came off AGAIN halfway over the Forth Road Bridge.

The Forth Bridges

Painters have to work continuously on the rail bridge. When they reach the end, it is time to start again!

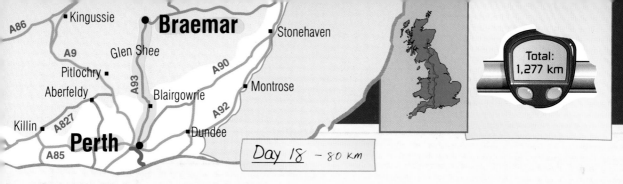

Day 18 – 80 km

Past Blairgowrie, we suddenly found ourselves in the Grampian mountains. We cycled all the way up Glenshee, which was our first Highland glen. It was a long steady climb to the highest point on the Cairnwell Pass (932 metres). There were ski slopes on both sides of the road and distant views of the Grampian mountains to the north. Then it was downhill all the way to Braemar – 12 km of bliss! – with mountains all around us and a tumbling river running alongside.

Glenshee taken from the Cairnwell Pass.

Glenshee Snowsport!

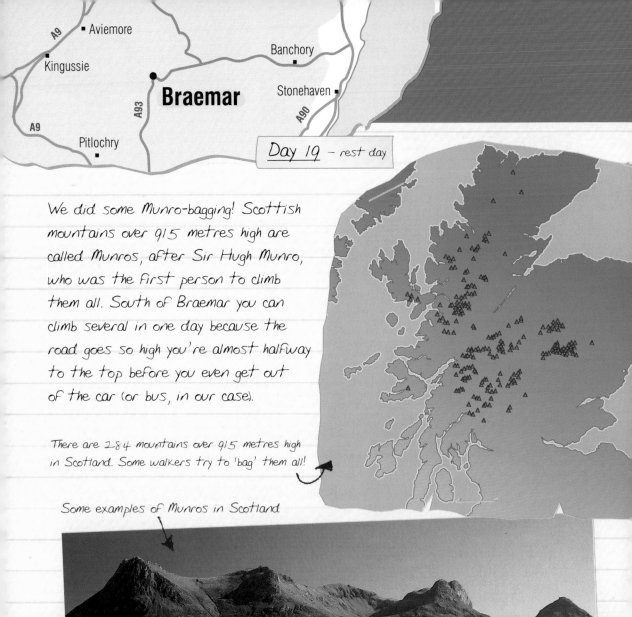

A9 • Aviemore

• Kingussie

• Banchory

Braemar

A93

Stonehaven •

A90

A9

• Pitlochry

We did some Munro-bagging! Scottish mountains over 915 metres high are called Munros, after Sir Hugh Munro, who was the first person to climb them all. South of Braemar you can climb several in one day because the road goes so high you're almost halfway to the top before you even get out of the car (or bus, in our case).

There are 284 mountains over 915 metres high in Scotland. Some walkers try to 'bag' them all!

Some examples of Munros in Scotland

Day 20 – 61 km

The road along Royal Deeside, past Balmoral Castle is flat and is not very busy. There was woodland on either side, so we didn't get a good view of the castle.

Balmoral Castle

After that, we were in the hills again. We passed Corgarff Castle, standing all on its own, and went on to the Lecht road, which is one of the highest roads in Britain, reaching a height of over 600 metres. From here we had great views of the Cairngorm mountains to the south.

We stayed at the youth hostel in Tomintoul, which is one of the highest villages in Britain.

Tomintoul youth hostel
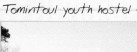

Corgarff Castle isn't quite as grand as Balmoral.

23

The ride north from Tomintoul was very pretty — high hills covered in purple heather, and plantations of dark green fir trees. We stopped for a tour of the whisky distillery at Glenlivet. The guide told us it is good whisky country because there is plenty of clean mountain water and it isn't far from barley country. We saw the barley fields as we cycled on through Strath Spey.

Then we crossed another stretch of high moorland which felt very empty and remote, before coming down into Forres on the wide, flat, sandy edge of the Moray Firth.

Welcome to the Glenlivet Distillery

THE GLENLIVET

The Moray Firth

A835

A9
Alness
Moray Firth
nasheen
Beauly Firth
A96
Forres
Keith
Inverness
Culloden
Moor
A9
Loch Ness

Total:
1,443 km

Day 22 – 49 km

↑
Culloden Moor

THE BATTLE
OF CULLODEN
WAS FOUGHT ON THIS MOOR
16TH APRIL 1746.

THE GRAVES OF THE
GALLANT HIGHLANDERS
WHO FOUGHT FOR
SCOTLAND & PRINCE CHARLIE
ARE MARKED BY THE NAMES
OF THEIR CLANS.

We started on flat roads near the coast, and then headed inland across Culloden Moor where a big battle took place in 1746. We visited the battlefield. More than 1,500 men were killed there in a dawn ambush, and the dead were buried in mass graves with rough stones bearing the names of each clan. It was a very bleak and eerie place.

After that, it was downhill all the way to Inverness, which is right on the sea at the head of Loch Ness.

Inverness

Alness
A9
Achnasheen
Moray Firth
A96
Forres

A9
Loch Ness

Inverness
Fort William
Edinburgh
Glasgow

Loch Ness is the longest loch in Scotland.
Its valley is called the Great Glen. You
can take a boat all the way down the
Great Glen from Inverness in the east
to Fort William in the west, through a
series of lakes joined by the Caledonian
Canal.

Loch Ness
Inverness
'The Great Glen'
Loch Oich
Loch Lochy
Fort William

We had a walk and tried to spot the Loch Ness monster.
We ate a Nessie Burger in a café. The man said it was made
of monster-meat, but they tasted like beef-burger to me.

Could this be Nessie?

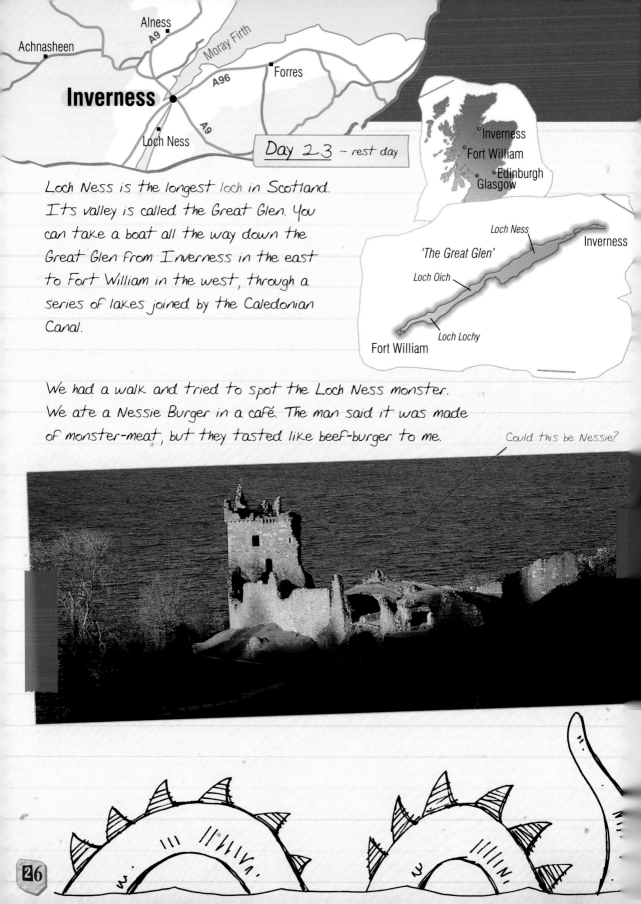

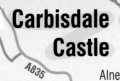

Carbisdale Castle

Dornoch Firth

A9

A835

Alness •

Moray Firth

chnasheen

Beauly Firth

chewe

A9

Forres •

Inverness •

Total:
1,528 km

Day 24 - 85 Km

We went over the bridge across the Moray Firth and along the north shore of the Beauly Firth. The road was flat, and we took our time, stopping to watch the dolphins.

> These dolphins in the Beauly Firth are the most northerly population in the world. Unfortunately, their numbers are threatened by pollution.

The water was VERY cold!

Then it was another climb up on to a long flat stretch of high moorland. We stopped for a rest on Struie Hill at a place called "Millionaire's View". From there, we could see right across the Dornoch Firth, with its long sandy beaches, and the high mountains beyond.

Millionaire's view

27

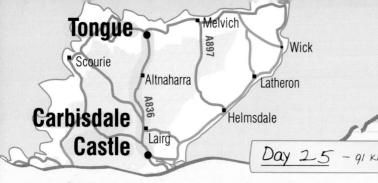

Tongue
Melvich
Wick
Scourie
Altnaharra
Latheron
A897
A836
Carbisdale Castle
Helmsdale
Lairg

Total: 1,619 km

Day 25 - 91 km

We bought some food in Lairg because we knew there wouldn't be another shop for 65 km. Then we took the main A836 all the way to Tongue. It was fantastic cycling - a wide straight road with nothing on it, and only quite gentle ups and downs.

Carbisdale Castle is a youth hostel which is supposed to be haunted by a woman in white, but we were too tired after our long bike ride to stay up and look for her.

The area is called the Flow Country, and it's full of streams and ponds and bogs. But in the distance we could see the mountains of the far North, like Ben Hope and Ben Loyal, which look more dramatic than the round-topped mountains of the Cairngorms and the Grampians, because they rise from sea-level and stand alone.

The Flow Country

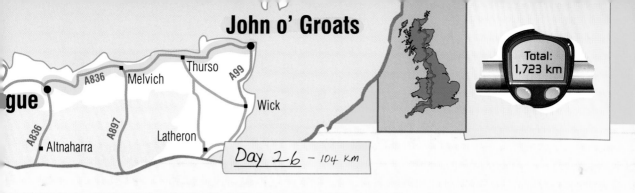

Day 26 – 104 km

We were on a main road again, but still with hardly any traffic on it. It followed the coast, which was very isolated and rugged, with empty white sandy beaches and dunes. We passed Dounreay, which was the first nuclear power station to be built in Britain.

For the last bit of the journey we cycled along minor roads again. The land was flat, so the roads were straight, and there were fences made of stone slabs sticking up out of the ground.

Dounreay Power Station

John o' Groats was completely different from Land's End. It didn't feel like a tourist resort, and there were far fewer people about. There was a proper village with a small school. We could see the Orkneys, out on the horizon.

We bought a postcard that told the story of how John o' Groats got its name.

John o' Groats is named after John de Groot, a Dutchman, who ran a ferry from the mainland to the Orkneys in the fifteenth century. He charged 4d (old pence) a trip, and the little 4d coin became known as a groat.

You can get an End to End Information Pack from the Cyclists' Touring Club (CTC).

CTC
Cotterell House
69 Meadrow
Godalming
Surrey
GU7 3HS

Or visit the CTC website:
www.ctc.org.uk

For information about youth hostels, write to:

Youth Hostels Association (England and Wales)
8 St Stephen's Hill
St Albans
Herts
AL1 2DY

Or visit the YHA website:
www.yha.org.uk

It was the best holiday ever - and I still can't believe I really did it!

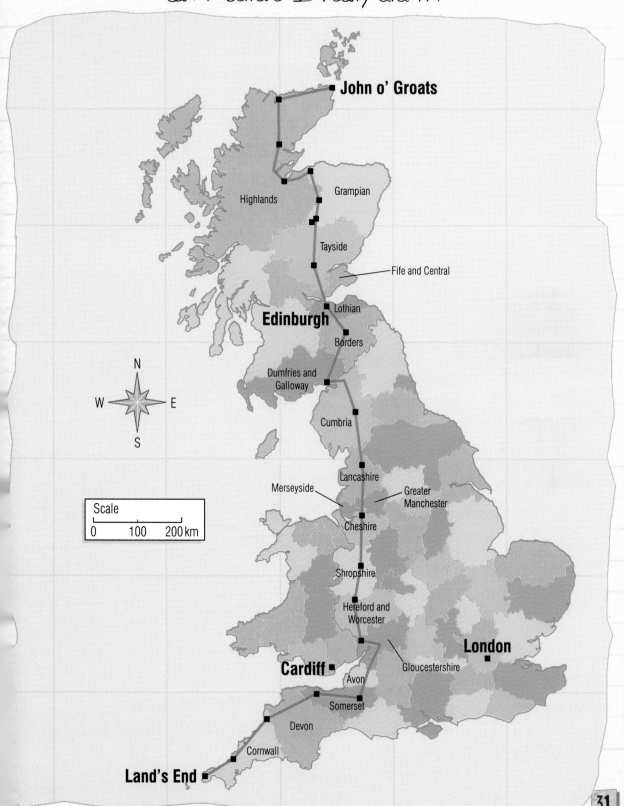

John o' Groats

Highlands

Grampian

Tayside

Fife and Central

Lothian

Edinburgh

Borders

Dumfries and Galloway

Cumbria

Lancashire

Merseyside

Greater Manchester

Cheshire

Shropshire

Hereford and Worcester

Gloucestershire

London

Cardiff

Avon

Somerset

Devon

Cornwall

Land's End

N
W · E
S

Scale
0   100   200 km

Glossary of geographical terms

ben* a high mountain or mountain peak

escarpment a long ridge with one steep side and one gently sloping side

estuary wide tidal mouth of a river

firth* an estuary

glen* a narrow valley

gorge a rocky valley, often with a river running through it

loch* a lake

marshland low land flooded in wet weather

moor open, unfarmed, hilly area

outcrop bare rock jutting up through the soil level

rural to do with the countryside

stalactite rock formation that looks like an icicle, caused by water dripping from the roof of a cave

stalagmite rock formation that looks like a mound or pillar, caused by water dripping on to the floor of a cave

strath* a broad valley

uplands high or hilly countryside

volcanic plug large mass of volcanic rock created when a volcano becomes inactive and the lava cools and solidifies

(*Scottish words)